Heart ♥ 2 HEART

Welcome to
**YOUR *dazzling*
TWO-WAY** BOOK
and JOURNAL!

Fill this half of the book with your
hopes, dreams, and heart's desires.
Flip the book over to find your
very own journal.

make
believe
ideas

I LOVE TO BE me!

Being me is wonderful – nobody does it better!

My name: Naomi Hilton

I rate my name __9__ /10

Other names I like to be called:
JoJo, Nana.

My birthday: April 11, 2008

My age today is __9__ years ~~8~~ months ~~8~~ days.

The place I was born: ~~8~~ 8

The time I was born: 11:4

Choose one word from each side of the heart, then combine these to create your fame name.

Violet Ocean
Matty Kelly Zara
Billie Charlie Louie
Liberty Alex
Taylor Tabby
Brooke
Edie
Bear

Star Sparkle
Dazzle-Dew Diamond
Appleton Pickle Berry
Frost Valentine
Summer Grace
Heath Winter
Peardrop
Rose

Tape a picture of yourself here.

My fame name:
Taylor Winter

What I'd love to be famous for:
Writing a good book

My birthstone

Circle the birthstone for the month you were born.

 January
Garnet

 February
Amethyst

 March
Aquamarine

 April
Diamond

 May
Emerald

 June
Pearl

 July
Ruby

 August
Peridot

 September
Sapphire

 October
Opal

 November
Citrine

 December
Blue topaz

The five best things about me:

1. I'm hilarous
2. teachers love me
3. I'm great at writing
4. I'm great at vocabulary
5. I have an intresting personality.

My eye color: hazel
My hair color: Brown
My height: 4' 7
My shoe size: Size 3

A little known fact about me:
I LOVE WRITING!

I ♥ me!

Where I live:
1843 South Knoh

The people I live with:
Mom, dad, Camille

My favorite place in the entire world is:
home

My favorite day of the year is:
December 25th
because It's chritmas and you get presents!

A drawing of my home

My favorite day of the week is:
Friday
because because the next day is Saterday and sunday weekends!

Five things I love about the people I live with:
1 there hilareus
2 they help me when I'm sick
3 consfort me if I hada/bad day
4 they love me
5 they are fun to play board games with

MY PERFECT day

At 9 o'clock …

at School working
on my work.

At 11 o'clock …

at lunch

At 1 o'clock …

doing math
which is no
fun.

At 3 o'clock …

chillaxing with
my book

At 5 o'clock …

eating dinner
I like to eat
dinner early.

At 7 o'clock …

chillaxing with
my book.

THE COLOR OF MY heart

Mark the five hearts that contain the things you like best. Next, note which color you have chosen more of to see what the color of your heart says about you!

Reading

Choir

Practical jokes

Movies

Crafts

Girl Scouts

Puzzles

Drama club

Shopping

Sleepovers

Swimming

Poetry

After-school clubs

Concerts

Volunteering

Playing an instrument

Team sports

Parties

Camping

Keeping a diary

Dancing

Dog walking

Drawing

Amusement parks

pink hearts
than any other:

You are loyal and dependable. People love spending time with you because you're always there for them.

purple hearts
than any other:

You are adventurous and always think of fun things to do. You can make anyone smile and are the life of any party.

blue hearts
than any other:

You are caring, creative, and like nothing more than giving thoughtful gifts, especially ones you made yourself. You can also write great stories and songs.

If you end up with two hearts of one color and two of another, choose the word that best describes you and use the color of its heart to reveal the color of your heart.

ways to my *heart*

Mark your choices in the circles.

Do you prefer . . .

● popcorn	OR	chocolate ○
● strawberries	OR	bananas ○
○ hashtags	OR	emotis ○
● kittens	OR	tigers ○
	depends	
○ pool	OR	beach ○
● dancing	OR	singing ○
● sleepovers	OR	movies ○
	depends	
○ fruit	OR	vegetables ○
● ocean view	OR	mountain view ○
	depends (don't like either)	
○ skiing	OR	snorkeling ○
● shopping for clothes	OR	shopping for gadgets ○
● crafting	OR	playing sports ○

I ♥ ALL ABOUT ME

5 words to describe me:
- funny
- 1081
- kind
- friendly
- caring

5 people I admire:
- Mom
- Dad
- grandma
- pop pop
- NaNa

5 things I'm grateful for:
- having friends
- a weathy family
- a healthy family
- people who love me
- caring teachers

5 happy memories:
- being picked for safty patrol
- teachers saying I'm a good writer
- teachers loving me
- meeting ellie
- meeting margan

5 people I would share my secrets with:
- Ellie
- Dad
- Mom
- Hayden
- camille (sometimes!)

5 top hobbies:
-
-
-
-
-

TREE OF

hearts

mem9..............

....

....

....

my family

Fill the leaves with the names
of your **family members**. If you want,
include the names of all the **people you
live with**, as well as your **pets**.

Fill in these pages with a friend.
Write your names, and then
take turns completing the quiz.

Heart 2

Name:

Oldest person in my family
....

Person with the most unusual talent
Camille crarp her A BCs ....

Sportiest person
....

Funniest person
....

Person with the most unusual name
....

Best dancer
....

Oldest pet in my family
....

The person I am most like
....

I HEART my family

Oldest person in my family

....

Person with the most unusual talent

....

Sportiest person

....

Funniest person

....

Person with the most unusual name

....

Best dancer

....

Oldest pet in my family

....

The person I am most like

....

Name:

never have we ever

Complete this quiz with a friend. Each time you answer **yes to a question, draw a heart** in the box below your name. **Count your hearts,** and write your total at the bottom. The **more similar** you and your friend's results, the **more you have in common.**

Have you ever . . .

	Name	Name
been to a pop concert?		
visited another country?		
stayed awake all night?		
been on a boat?		
gone surfing?		
been on safari?		
worn a ball gown?		
stayed at a hotel?		
knit a hat?		
sung in a play?		
seen a real crocodile?		
met a celebrity?		
watched a 3-D movie?		
TOTAL:		

heartart

A STRING OF HEARTS

Make a pretty string of hearts
to decorate your room.

1 Cut out 8 pieces of stiff red paper,
approximately 3 in x 3 in
(8 cm x 8 cm). Fold them in half.
Draw half a heart on each one and
then a smaller half-heart inside it.

2 Cut out the big and
small hearts.

3 Tape some thread along the fold of a large heart.
Then add the other large hearts to the same thread.

4 Tape a small heart in the center
of each large heart.

5 Write some of the things you love on
the big hearts. These could be people,
places, possessions, TV shows, food,
or anything else!

cats Dad

ways to my *heart*

Mark your choices in the circles.

Do you prefer . . .

○ chic	OR	casual ○
○ sweater	OR	vest top ○
○ ponytail	OR	braids ○
○ glitter	OR	sequins ○
○ stripes	OR	polka dots ○
○ pastel	OR	neon ○
○ sandals	OR	flip-flops ○
○ baseball cap	OR	beanie hat ○
○ tote bag	OR	handbag ○
○ scarves	OR	turtlenecks ○
○ gloves	OR	mittens ○
○ high heels	OR	sneakers ○

I  FASHION

5 most-loved things
in my closet:

- ....
- ....
- ....
- ....
- ....

5 favorite accessories:

- ....
- ....
- ....
- ....
- ....

5 top hairstyles:

- ....
- ....
- ....
- ....
- ....

My dream party outfit
would look like this.

Fill in these pages with a friend.
Write your names, and then
take turns completing the quiz.

Heart 2

Name:

Best class

....

Best after-school activity

....

Favorite teacher

....

Favorite thing about school

....

One thing I would change about school

....

Lunch meal I like best

....

Funniest thing I ever saw at school

....

My best moment

....

HEART my school

Best class
....

Best after-school activity
....

Favorite teacher
....

Favorite thing about school
....

One thing I would change about school
....

Lunch meal I like best
....

Funniest thing I ever saw at school
....

My best moment
....

Name:

TREE OF hearts

my friends

Fill the leaves with the
names of your friends and
other **people you like.**

ways to my *heart*

Mark your choices in the circles.

Would you prefer . . . ?

○ to study French **OR** to study Spanish ○

○ to start school at 6 a.m. **OR** to finish school at 6 p.m. ○

○ to have a weeklong science class **OR** to have a weeklong art class ○

○ to have a sandwich for lunch everyday **OR** to have a burger for lunch everyday ○

○ if science class was canceled **OR** if music class was canceled ○

○ to be the principal **OR** to be a teacher ○

○ to work in a group **OR** to work alone ○

○ to be a top student **OR** to be a sports star ○

○ to go to a school for the arts **OR** to go to a school for geniuses ○

○ to be the smartest in your class **OR** to be the funniest in your class ○

○ to wear a tracksuit to school **OR** to wear a suit to school ○

○ to learn to sing **OR** to learn to dance ○

I  MY HEART'S DESIRES

These are my favorite things:

Person
....

Snack
....

Season
....

Book
....

Color
....

Movie
....

Song
....

Animal
....

Country
....

School subject
....

Fill in these pages with a friend. Write your names, and then take turns completing the quiz.

If you were stranded on a desert island and could only have one thing from each category, what would you choose?

Heart 2

Name:

Item from your bedroom

Item of furniture

Item from your kitchen

Electronic item

Book

Game

Outfit accessory

Food treat

HEART desert-island dreams

Item from your bedroom

....

Item of furniture

....

Item from your kitchen

....

Electronic item

....

Book

....

Game

....

Outfit accessory

....

Food treat

....

Name:

TREE OF

hearts

the most
wonderful times
of the year

Fill the leaves with **the birthdays, celebrations,** and other times of the year that are **closest to your heart.**

ways to my *heart*

Would you prefer . . .

Mark your choices in the circles.

- ○ surfing **OR** snowboarding ○
- ○ running **OR** cycling ○
- ○ an apartment **OR** a hotel ○
- ○ swimming **OR** sailing ○
- ○ summer **OR** winter ○
- ○ to travel the world **OR** to travel into space ○
- ○ a city break **OR** a country retreat ○
- ○ a safari **OR** mountain hiking ○
- ○ a ship **OR** an airplane ○
- ○ swimming with dolphins **OR** snorkeling with turtles ○
- ○ to zip-line over a forest **OR** to scuba dive ○
- ○ to stay in an arctic igloo **OR** to stay in a tropical tree house ○

I  MY BUCKET LIST

5 places I'd like to visit:
- ....
- ....
- ....
- ....
- ....

5 sports I'd like to learn:
- ....
- ....
- ....
- ....
- ....

5 activities I'd like to try:
- ....
- ....
- ....
- ....
- ....

5 movies I'd like to see:
- ....
- ....
- ....
- ....
- ....

5 people I'd like to meet:
- ....
- ....
- ....
- ....
- ....

5 skills I'd like to learn:
- ....
- ....
- ....
- ....
- ....

Fill in these pages with a friend.
Write your names, and then
take turns completing the quiz.

Heart 2

Name:

Name I would choose if I had to change mine
....

Favorite celebrity
....

Best gift I've ever received
....

An animal I would like to be
....

Most embarrassing moment at school
....

A book character I would love to have as a friend
....

The silliest excuse I have ever given
....

My funniest habit
....

HEART fun secrets

Name I would choose if I had to change mine

....

Favorite celebrity

....

Best gift I've ever received

....

An animal I would like to be

....

Most embarrassing moment at school

....

A book character I would love to have as a friend

....

The silliest excuse I have ever given

....

My funniest habit

....

Name:

TREE OF

hearts

my
favorite places

in the world

Fill the leaves with the names
of the **countries, towns, cities,**
and **places** you **love the most.**

heartart

JAR OF HEARTS

Fill a jar with secret notes about the things you love. They could be people, places, memories, or anything else. Then, every time you discover something new that you love, add another note to your jar.

You will need:

- Scissors
- A pencil
- A jar
- Decorations for your jar

1 Carefully cut out the mini notes on the next three pages of this book.

2 Write one thing that you love on each note. It might be your pet or an activity you love to do on the weekends.

3 After writing each note, roll it up and tuck it into your jar for safekeeping.

4 Decorate the jar with ribbons, hearts, glitter, and anything else you like.

I love . . .

I like . . .

This page and the next two pages contain the mini notes needed for your jar of hearts.

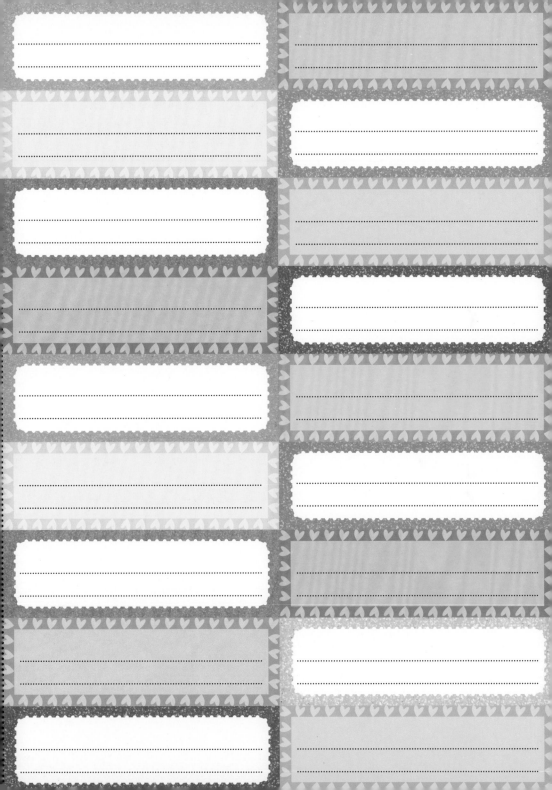

I  MY YEAR

5 best summer activities:

- ....
- ....
- ....
- ....
- ....

5 funny memories:
- ....
- ....
- ....
- ....
- ....

5 best winter activities:

- ....
- ....
- ....
- ....
- ....

5 special occasions this year:
- ....
- ....
- ....
- ....
- ....

5 top weekend activities:

- ....
- ....
- ....
- ....
- ....

5 best friends:

- ....
- ....
- ....
- ....
- ....

Fill in these pages with a friend. Write your names, and then take turns completing the quiz.

Heart 2

Name:

Farthest place I've ever traveled to
....

Latest bedtime
....

Earliest morning
....

Longest car journey
....

Greatest school achievement
....

Longest phone call
....

Tastiest food I ever ate
....

Longest time away from home
....

HEART extremes

Farthest place I've ever traveled to

....

Latest bedtime

....

Earliest morning

....

Longest car journey

....

Greatest school achievement

....

Longest phone call

....

Tastiest food I ever ate

....

Longest time away from home

....

Name:

never have we ever

Complete this quiz with a friend. Each time you answer **yes to a question, draw a heart** in the box below your name. **Count your hearts**, and write your total at the bottom. The **more similar** you and your friend's results, the **more you have in common.**

Have you ever . . .

	Name	Name
learned to play the piano?		
volunteered for charity?		
painted a portrait?		
been on a plane?		
eaten escargot? (snails)		
written a song?		
sung in the shower?		
been in a hot-air balloon?		
knit a scarf?		
watched TV all day?		
got an A for a school assignment?		
run a mile?		
owned a pet?		

TOTAL:

SUPER
Secret
POCKET

CUT ALONG HERE

TAPE HERE

WELCOME to YOUR
SUPER *Secret* POCKET!

Carefully **cut along the dotted line,**
and then **tape the pages together.**

Now you have a special pocket
for storing your **secret notes.**

Make sure you **fix the top of the pocket
with a paper clip** before you flip
the book over.

TAPE HERE

TAPE HERE

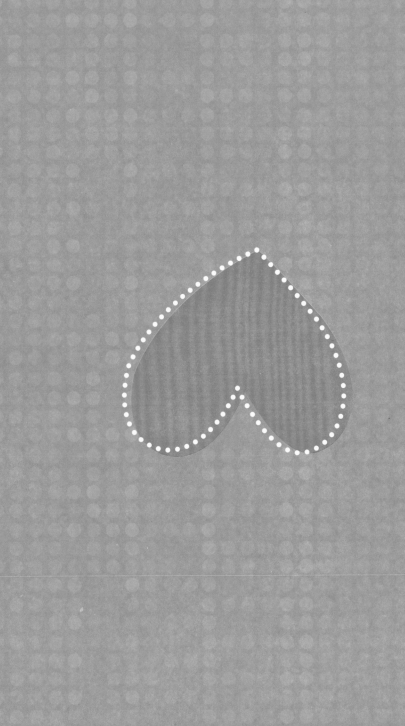

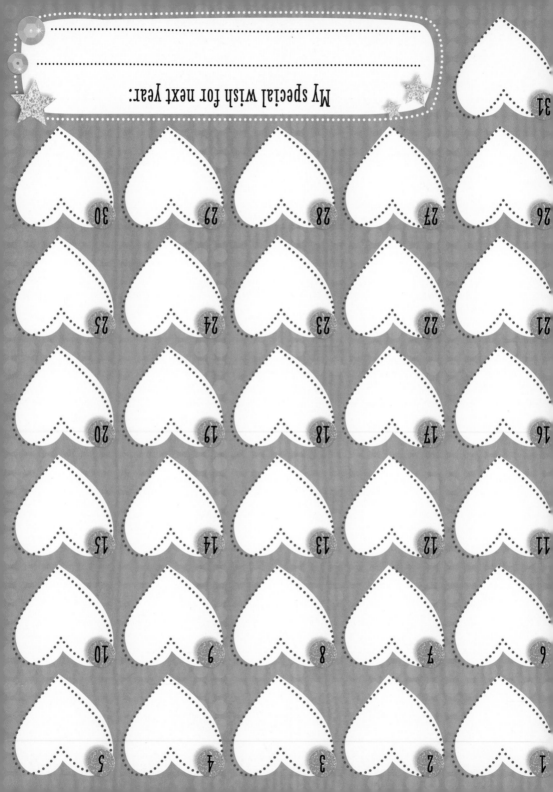

My special wish for next year:

December

Three things I'm looking
forward to this month:

1 ....
2 ....
3 ....

Three things I loved
about this month:

1 ....
2 ....
3 ....

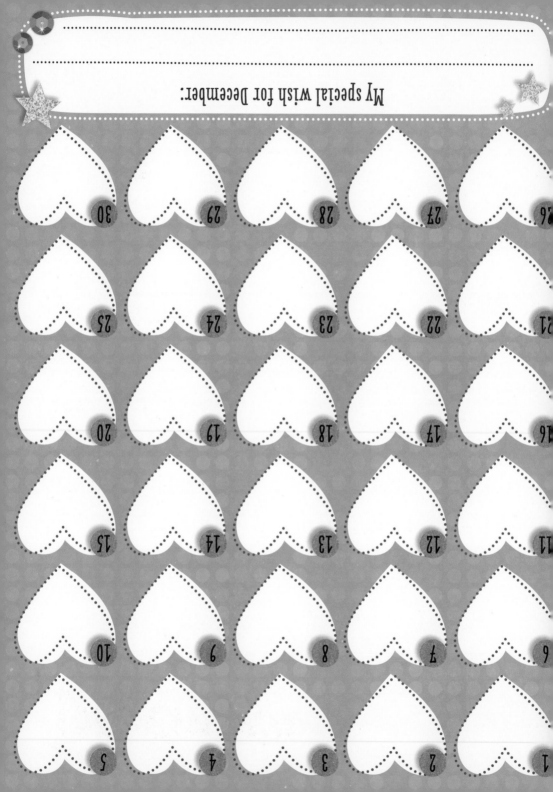

My special wish for December:

30 29 28 27 26

25 24 23 22 21

20 19 18 17 16

15 14 13 12 11

10 9 8 7 6

5 4 3 2

Three things I loved
about this month:

3
2
1

Three things I'm looking
forward to this month:

3
2
1

November

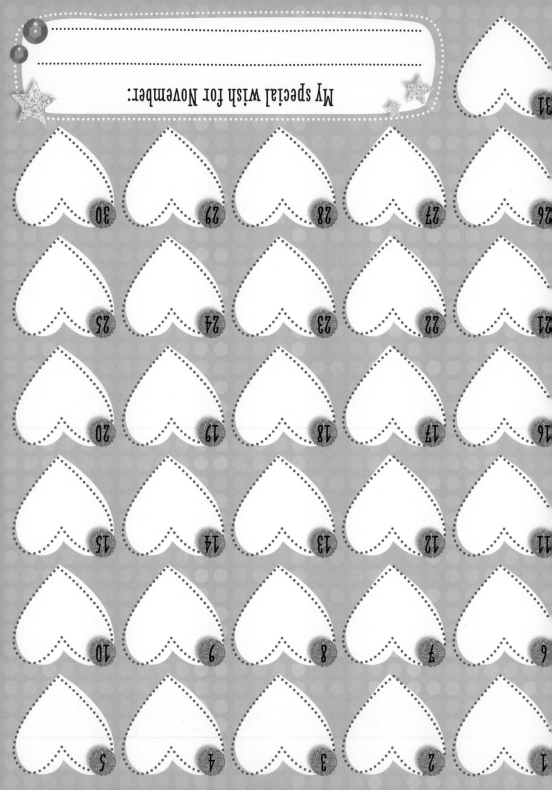

My special wish for November:

31
30 29 28 27 26
25 24 23 22 21
20 19 18 17 16
15 14 13 12 11
10 9 8 7 6
5 4 3 2

October

Three things I'm looking forward to this month:

1. ....
2. ....
3. ....

Three things I loved about this month:

1. ....
2. ....
3. ....

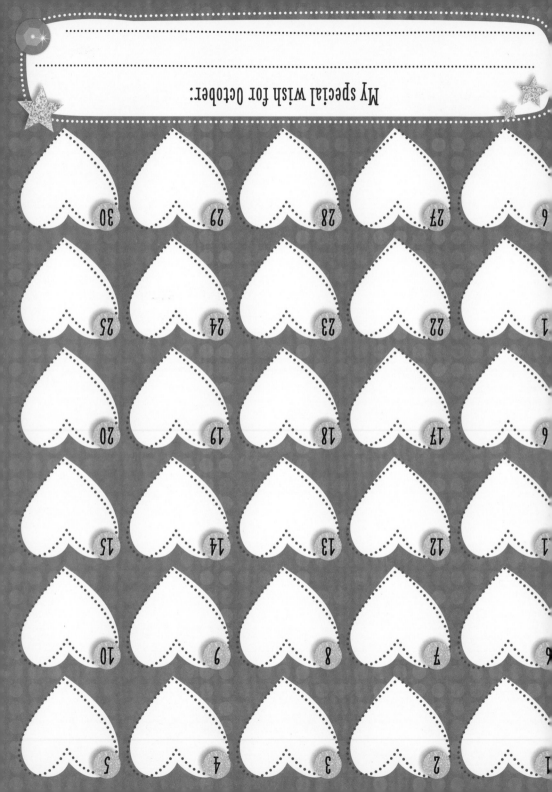

September

Three things I'm looking
forward to this month:

1 ....
2 ....
3 ....

Three things I loved
about this month:

1 ....
2 ....
3 ....

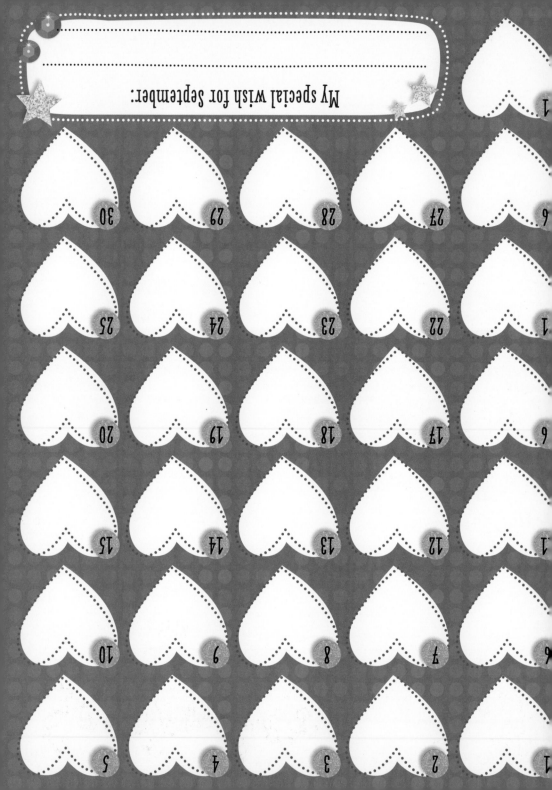

My special wish for September:

August

Three things I'm looking forward to this month:

1 ....
2 ....
3 ....

Three things I loved about this month:

1 ....
2 ....
3 ....

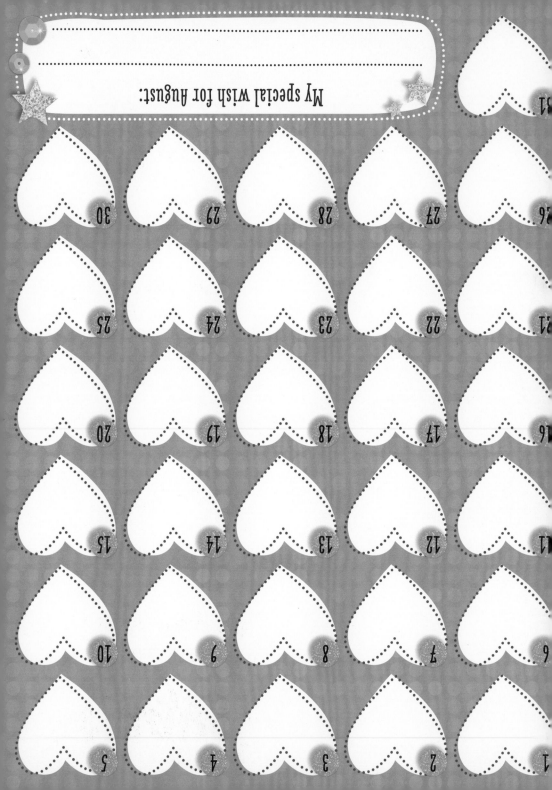

My special wish for August:

31

30   29   28   27   26

25   24   23   22   21

20   19   18   17   16

15   14   13   12   11

10   9   8   7   6

5   4   3   2

July

Three things I'm looking forward to this month:

1 ....

2 ....

3 ....

Three things I loved about this month:

1 ....

2 ....

3 ....

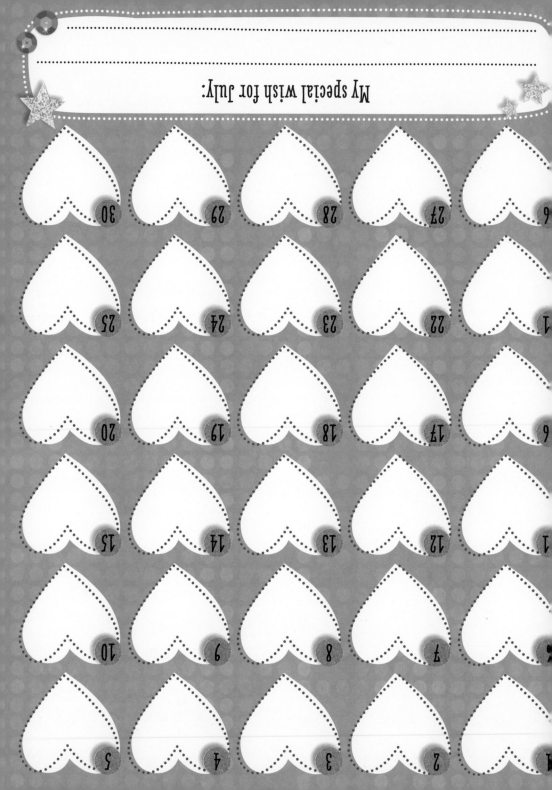

My special wish for July:

Three things I loved
about this month:

1

2

3

....
....
....

Three things I'm looking
forward to this month:

1

2

3

....
....
....

June

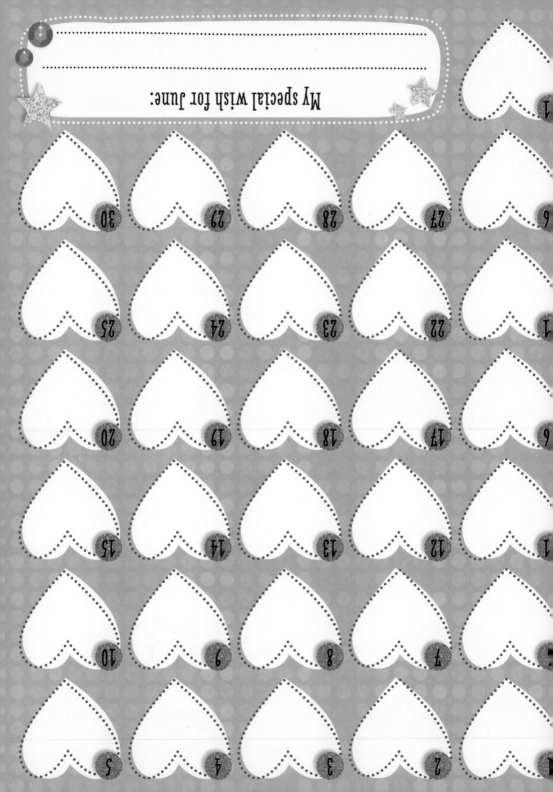

My special wish for June:

Three things I loved
about this month:

1
2
3

··
··
··

Three things I'm looking
forward to this month:

1
2
3

··
··
··

May

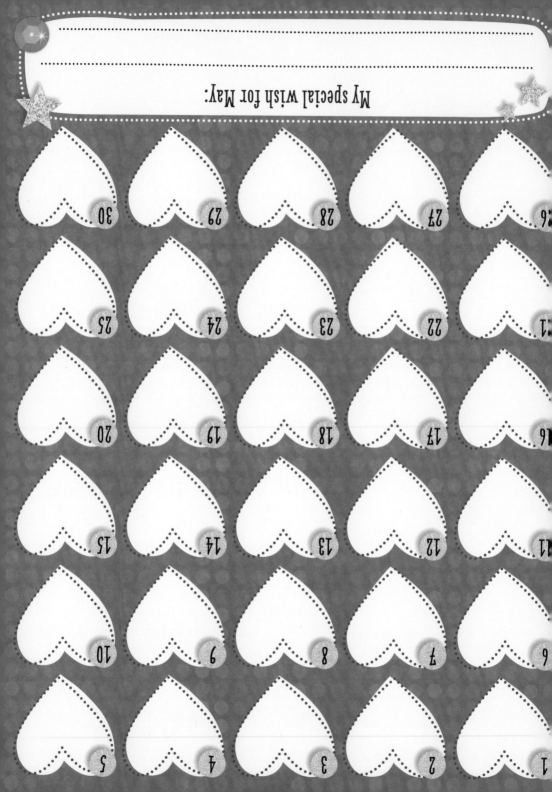

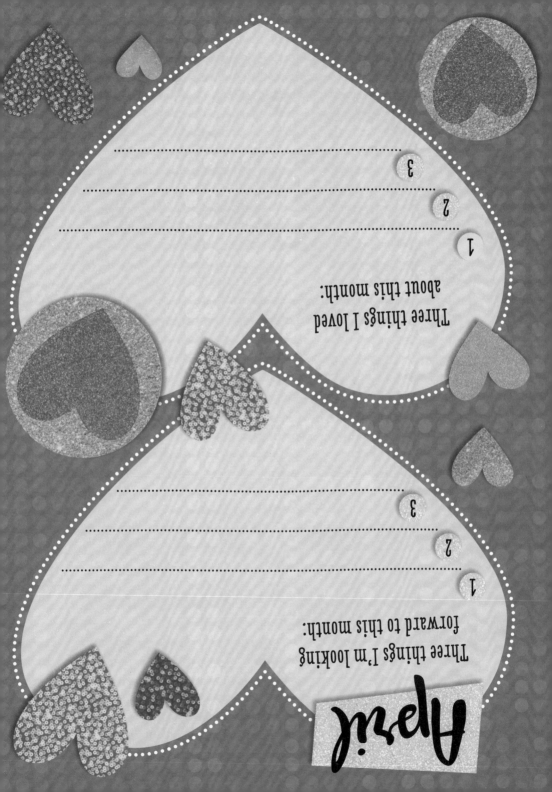

Three things I loved
about this month:

1
2
3

Three things I'm looking
forward to this month:

1
2
3

April

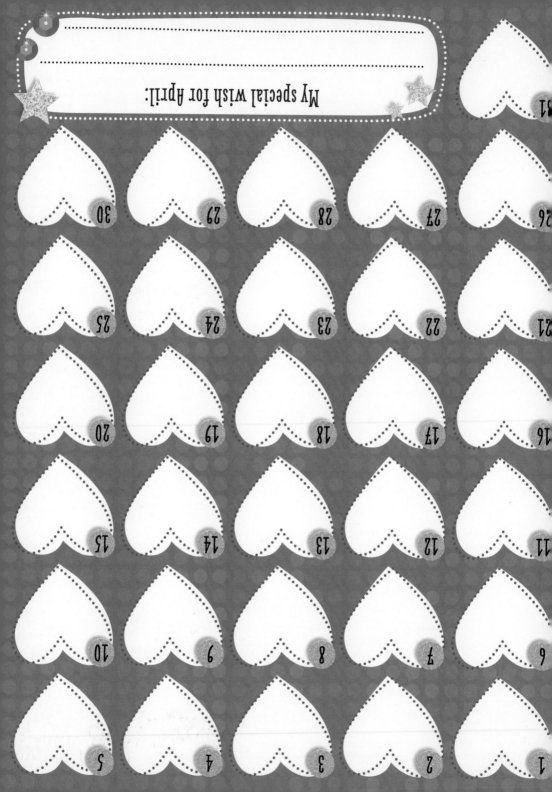

My special wish for April:

Three things I loved about this month:

1

2

3

Three things I'm looking forward to this month:

1

2

3

March

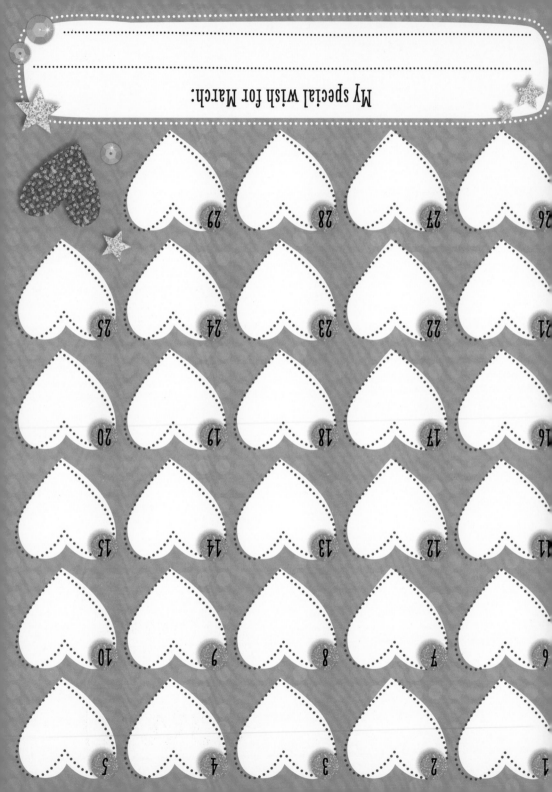

My special wish for March:

29 28 27 26

25 24 23 22 21

20 19 18 17 16

15 14 13 12 11

10 9 8 7 6

5 4 3 2 1

February

Three things I'm looking forward to this month:

1 ....

2 ....

3 ....

Three things I loved about this month:

1 ....

2 ....

3 ....

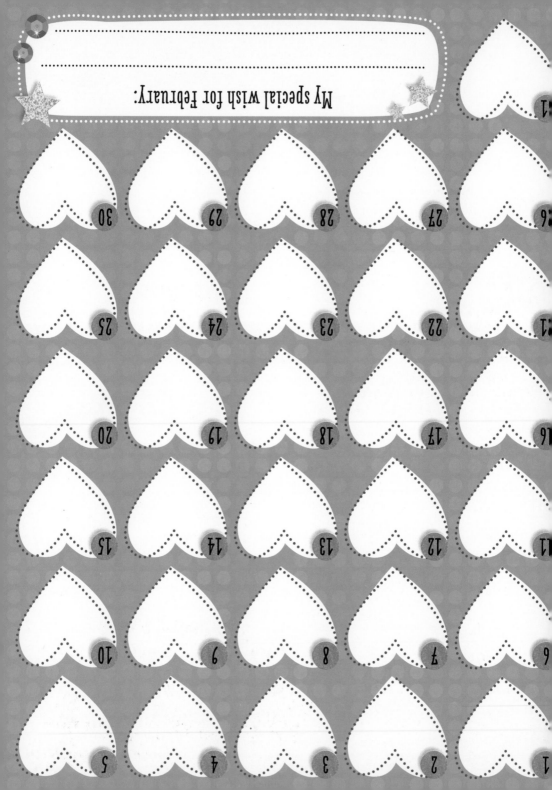

My special wish for February:

31

30 29 28 27 26

25 24 23 22 21

20 19 18 17 16

15 14 13 12 11

10 9 8 7 6

5 4 3 2 1

January

Three things I'm looking
forward to this month:

1
....

2
....

3
....

Three things I loved
about this month:

1
....

2
....

3
....

For each month, there are two hearts on the left-hand page.
Fill in the first heart at the start of the month,
and fill in the second heart at the end of the month.

♥ ♥ ♥

Ways you could fill in the daily hearts:
• Record any fun or important things that are planned.
• Jot down what happened each day and how you feel about it.

Mia is my new BFF!

30

Gym starts today!

HEART
JOURNAL

Heart 2 HEART